Political & Economic Systems

MONARCHY

Richard Tames

www.heinemann.co.uk/library

Visit our website to find out more information about Heinemann Library books.

To order:

 Phone 44 (0) 1865 888066

Send a fax to 44 (0) 1865 314091

 Visit the Heinemann Bookshop at www.heinemann.co.uk/library to browse our catalogue and order online.

First published in Great Britain by Heinemann Library,
Halley Court, Jordan Hill, Oxford OX2 8EJ,
a division of Reed Educational and Professional Publishing Ltd.
Heinemann is a registered trademark of Reed Educational and Professional Publishing Ltd.

OXFORD MELBOURNE AUCKLAND
JOHANNESBURG BLANTYRE GABORONE
IBADAN PORTSMOUTH (NH) USA CHICAGO

Designed by AMR
Illustrated by Art Construction
Originated by Dot Gradations
Printed in Hong Kong by South China Printing

ISBN 0 431 12430 2 (hardback)
06 05 04 03 02
10 9 8 7 6 5 4 3 2 1

British Library Cataloguing in Publication Data

Tames, Richard
  Monarchy. – (Political & economic systems)
  1. Monarchy – Juvenile literature
  I. Title
  321.6

Acknowledgements
The publishers would like to thank the following for permission to reproduce photographs:
Bridgeman: pp. 17, 18, 20, 25; Bridgeman/Bibliotheque Nationale: p. 27; Bridgeman/British Library: p. 12; Bridgeman/Fitzwilliam Museum, University of Cambridge: p. 33; Bridgeman/Musee de Picardie: p. 5; Bridgeman/Winchester Cathedral: p. 13; Corbis: p. 55; Corbis/Archivo Iconografico: pp. 9, 23; Corbis/Bettmann: pp. 38, 45; Corbis/Dave Bartruff: p. 36; Corbis/Quadrillion: p. 49; Corbis/Ric Ergenbright: p. 30; Corbis/Roger Wood: p. 16; Corbis/Steve Raymer: p. 41; Corbis/Sygma/Anderson Thorne: p. 52; Hulton Archive: p. 47; National Trust Scotland/A. Smith: p. 24; Popperfoto: p. 31; Popperfoto/Reuters: p. 14.

Cover photograph: Queen Elizabeth II at the opening of Parliament, UK, reproduced with permission of Rex.

Every effort has been made to contact copyright holders of any material reproduced in this book. Any omissions will be rectified in subsequent printings if notice is given to the publishers.

Our thanks to Christopher Gibb for his comments in the preparation of this book.

Contents

1 Death of a king, death of kingship 4

2 Rulers and rebels 6

3 Monarchy or republic? 11

4 Sacred kingship – kings as gods, kings and God 16

5 War and peace 22

6 Ruling – right and wrong 27

7 Kings under control 33

8 Kings in control 41

9 Monarchies today and tomorrow 46

10 So, what is monarchy? 53

*Map showing world monarchies at the
turn of the 21st century* 54

Timeline 56

Further reading, sources & websites 58

Monarchies today 59

Glossary 61

Index 64

Any words appearing in the text in bold, **like this**,
are explained in the glossary.

The dates that follow the names of kings and queens
in the text are the dates of the monarch's reign.

Death of a king, death of kingship

On 20 January 1649 a sad-looking man, weary but proud, entered ancient Westminster Hall in London to face his accusers. He was Charles I, King of England, Scotland and Ireland – and he was on trial for his life. Speaking softly and with a stammer, he remained cool and dignified. He stood accused of making war on his own people. He would be tried by the very men who had crushed his armies in battle.

Charles declared no court on earth had the right to try him. He believed that for his conduct as king he would answer directly to God and to God alone. He therefore sat silent throughout his trial. The **verdict** was guilty and the sentence was death. 'Charles Stuart, for levying war against the present parliament and people therein represented, should be put to death by beheading as a **tyrant**, **traitor**, murderer and public enemy of the good people of this land.'

On the date fixed for his execution, 30 January 1649, Charles asked for an extra shirt. 'The season is so sharp as probably may make me shake, which some observers may imagine proceeds from fear.' Charles did not fear death.

The site of the king's execution – the magnificent Banqueting House of Whitehall Palace – was chosen to send out a message. It represented the pride and power of Britain's monarchy. Charles had had its ceiling painted by the famous artist, Peter Paul Rubens. The picture showed the king's father, King James I (1603–25), being carried up to Heaven by angels as a reward for his wise and just rule. Charles's excutioners ensured, therefore, that almost the last thing he saw on earth was a painting praising a monarchy which would end minutes later with his own death.

Charles stepped out through a window of the Banqueting House, onto a **scaffold** put up outside. He declared that the people had the right to be governed by laws protecting their lives, liberty and property but that making those laws was a matter for the monarch not the people.

'A subject and a sovereign are clear different things.' He then knelt, prayed and waited calmly for the axe.

Parliament proclaimed that not only was the king dead but so was monarchy as a system of government. England would now become a **republic**. It was known as the Commonwealth.

The power of kings

'The power of kings ... is nothing else but what only is ... committed to them in trust from the people to the common good of them all, in whom the power yet remains ... and cannot be taken from them.'

John Milton, Parliamentarian and poet

This painting, by a Flemish artist, depicts the execution of Charles I, with a portrait of the king on the left. The king's head was struck off with a single blow and held up to the crowd with the words 'Behold the head of a traitor!'.

2 Rulers and rebels

After 1649 parliament tried to govern without a king. With no clear leadership there was drift and muddle. There were **rebellions** in Ireland and Scotland which strengthened the importance of the army. In 1653, less than five years after the abolition of the monarchy, the army general Oliver Cromwell became Lord Protector. Cromwell was a **military dictator**, but lived at Hampton Court palace like a king, sat on a **throne**, had his head put on coins as kings did and, when he died, he was buried in Westminster Abbey like a king. Cromwell's son Richard became the next Lord Protector, but found ruling too difficult. George Monck, a senior general, then recalled parliament. This invited the late king's son to come back from **exile** and rule as Charles II. England's experiment as a **republic** was over.

Monarchy was restored, but a monarchy controlled by an elected parliament. The country had.been made to face the great problems of politics. By what right does a government govern? What are the rightful limits to the power of government? How can these limits be enforced? How can power be passed peacefully from one government to another?

Giving good government

The most common solution to the problem of government has been monarchy. Monarchy means rule by a single person, usually a king. The word comes from the Greek for 'alone' (*mono*) and 'to rule' (*archein*). Kings have based their claim to legitimacy – their right to rule – on several different principles. Most usually they claimed **descent** from a ruling family (**dynasty**) or even a god, less often by right of straightforward conquest or successful rebellion. Legitimacy is normally symbolically confirmed by a solemn ceremony such as a **coronation** in which the king is given a crown (from the Latin *corona*) as a mark of office. In theory, monarchy has the virtue of simplicity – one person gives the orders, so responsibility for good or bad government is clear. Continuity of government should be assured. When the king dies his son takes over, like inheriting a family business.

In practice it has not been so simple. However hard-working they are, monarchs cannot do everything that needs to be done. They need ministers to serve them as advisers, generals and officials to carry out their orders. They do not always have a son to succeed them. They can be challenged for power by ambitious ministers or members of their own family, especially when their rule seems to be failing the kingdom in some way. Usually when a ruler was deposed (overthrown) the successful plotter took the throne. In modern times deposition has often ended a monarchy altogether. In 1974 Emperor Haile Selassie of Ethiopia (1930–74) was deposed by the army, it was said in favour of his son the Crown Prince. Haile Selassie died mysteriously the next year and a military dictatorship took over, plunging the country into twenty years of **civil war**. In 1979 the ruler of Iran, Mohammad Reza Pahlavi (1941–79), was deposed by a revolution led by religious leaders and the country became an **Islamic** Republic.

In her own right

A queen is normally just the wife of a king. Her main duty is to produce a son to succeed him. In many countries law or custom barred a woman from succeeding to the throne. But there are many examples of queens who were stronger characters than their husbands and had more real power over government. When a king died leaving a boy as heir, the queen might rule as regent (rule for him) until he grew up. In ancient Egypt Queen Hatshepsut (1472–1458 BC) was regent for her nephew, but then had herself crowned as **pharaoh** and even wore a false beard, a symbol of kingly power, just like a male pharaoh. When Constantine VI of Byzantium grew up, his regent mother, Empress Irene (780–802), deposed and blinded him to rule in her own right until she was deposed in turn in AD 802. Catherine de Medici, who lived from 1519 to 1589, had three sons who were kings of France and was herself the real ruler during the reigns of the first two. From about 1500 onwards in parts of Europe it became possible for a queen to rule in her own right. In Japan, even today, this is still not allowed by law.

Who can be king?

Succession to a throne is often thought of as a straightforward matter, depending on **heredity**. When the king dies, his eldest son becomes king. To many people that is what defines monarchy as a system. In practice it has not always worked like that. Among German **tribes** fighting the Romans, the king was essentially a commander, so the best warrior was elected.

The Germanic custom of elected kings may have become limited to candidates from families famed for bravery or claiming descent from the gods. The **ancestry** of Queen Elizabeth II can be traced back to Cerdic, leader of a German war-band, who landed in England around AD 495. Cerdic himself claimed descent from Wodin, the supreme god of the Saxons and Vikings.

As Anglo-Saxons and other peoples adopted Christianity, another element was needed for proper **accession** to a throne – **coronation** by a Christian priest. This meant swearing to rule justly and defend the church, accepting symbols of power, such as a sword and **sceptre**, and being anointed with holy oil. In some kingdoms it became customary that a proper coronation could only be held at a particular place – in France at **Reims**, in Scotland at **Scone**.

In the Anglo-Saxon monarchy, the **hereditary** principle of son succeeding father became usual, but was flexibly applied. Because a king had to lead in battle, children often and women always were shut out from the succession, though the wives and mothers of kings often had great power behind the scenes. Only much later, when countries relied on full-time armies led by professional generals, was it possible for women to rule as queens in their own right.

Another problem arose if the ruler simply had no children, like Edward the Confessor (1042–66). His death led to a struggle for the throne between William of Normandy (the Conqueror), who claimed it had been promised to him, and Harold Godwinson, the most powerful landowner in England, who seized the throne for himself. He was killed in battle at Hastings in 1066 and the victor William became king in his place.

This is a panel from the Bayeux Tapestry, made in about 1080 to record the Norman conquest of England in 1066. William the Conqueror (1066–87) personally turned the tide of the decisive battle at Hastings to become the last successful foreign invader of England.

Henry I (1100–35) had at least twenty **illegitimate** children, but only a son born within marriage could lawfully succeed to the throne. Henry's only **legitimate** son was drowned in 1120. Henry persuaded the leading nobles to swear that they would accept his daughter Matilda as queen. When Henry died, Matilda's cousin Stephen (1135–54) broke his oath and seized the throne for himself. The result was civil war, until Stephen agreed to accept Matilda's son as his successor, Henry II (1154–89). In turn, Henry II died with two of his sons in armed rebellion against him.

Successful **rebellion** against the throne, as in the case of Henry VII (1485–1509) later added yet another requirement for rightful succession beside some claim to royal blood and coronation. Henry claimed that he had overthrown Richard III (1483–85) because he had murdered the rightful king, Richard's own nephew Edward V (1483), who was just a boy. Richard had also executed many nobles unlawfully and seized their lands. Henry VII got parliament to pass an Act confirming him as king, to show that the nation as a whole approved his rebellion as just.

Co-rulers

Even kings who rule wisely and stay sane and safe can still have problems ensuring that a competent successor takes over peacefully. One device, used for example in Japan, was co-rulership. Here the chosen **heir** takes on some of the duties of government or rules part of the kingdom, while the existing ruler moves into semi-retirement. One danger of co-ruling, though, is the heir becoming impatient for full power and rising in rebellion to overthrow his father.

③ Monarchy or republic?

Nowadays most of the world's governments are **republics**. A century ago most countries in the world were governed by monarchs. They were usually called 'King' or 'Queen' but other names were used. In Russia, the monarch was the 'Tsar', in Iran 'Shah' and in other parts of Asia the title was 'Rajah' or 'Khan'. A monarch ruling a large, **multi-ethnic** population was often styled 'Emperor'. Rulers of very small states might be called 'Prince' or 'Grand Duke'. In Europe, the monarchs were generally **constitutional**. This means the monarch's political power was limited by a **constitution**, a set of rules which sets out how the government works. The ruler had to govern in co-operation with a parliament elected by at least some of the ordinary people of their country.

Republics are governments headed by an elected president. A century ago, they were in the minority. The biggest was the USA. Latin American countries were also republics, which from time to time collapsed into **dictatorships**. Europe's only republics were Switzerland and France, which had had ten different kinds of monarchy or republic since 1789. Except for the USA, republics were mostly poor, and except for Switzerland, unstable as well.

Monarchy has been the most common form of government for most of human history. There are still over two dozen monarchies today. The monarchies of western Europe, the Commonwealth and Japan are **democratic** and constitutional. In Africa, Asia, the Middle East and the Pacific, monarchies are more often traditional or **tribal**. Obedience to the government depends on respect for the ruling family or sometimes belonging to their tribe. Some of these traditional rulers are trying to move towards more democratic forms of government.

This 14th-century painting shows King Solomon dictating his proverbs (wise sayings). The Hebrews of ancient Israel honoured King David as a great warrior and poet and his son, King Solomon, as a wise judge.

Monarchy, change and progress

Although nowadays most people in the world live in a republic, many will know something about monarchy from history, religion, literature and myth. Real history supplies the example of King Alfred (871–99), who would rather have spent his days in prayer and study than ruling. But he saved his kingdom, Wessex, from destruction, converted **pagan** Danish invaders to Christianity, founded England's first navy and first official history, organized the laws into a system and encouraged English as a language of learning.

The idea of monarchy comes from the distant past, but throughout its long history monarchy has often brought progress. Kings often united warring cities and regions into larger, stronger states. They battled to impose the same laws throughout their lands. They encouraged trade and industry. The UK, one of the world's oldest monarchies, was the first nation in the world to produce most of its wealth from modern industries.

This 19th-century statue of Alfred the Great is at Winchester, which was the capital of Wessex. Alfred believed a king should make his kingdom strong, prosperous, peaceful and law-abiding and is the only English king called 'the Great'.

Under Emperor Meiji (1867–1912) Japan, an even older monarchy, transformed itself in 40 years from backward isolation to become a major military and naval power. Foreign experts and western technology were brought in to modernize the armed forces and industry. The Emperor set a personal example by always wearing western-style clothes and visiting schools to show how important learning was to create a new Japan.

Republics have almost always come into existence after a monarchy has failed to manage a crisis, or collapsed outright, rather than because a republican form of government was positively wanted.

Top ten

The United Nations calculates a Human Development Index, ranking countries by a combination of income, health, **literacy**, civil liberties, treatment of minorities etc. to show their overall quality of life. The top ten nations include 8 monarchies and 2 republics. They are: **1** Canada **2** Norway **3** USA* **4** Australia **5** Iceland* **6** Sweden **7** Belgium **8** Netherlands **9** Japan **10** UK

(* = republic)

Kings do many things

The job description for a monarch has changed greatly over the centuries. In ancient monarchies, such as Egypt under the **pharaohs**, the ruler led the most important religious ceremonies, commanded the army in war, dealt with foreign rulers and acted as judge and law-maker. He also made sure that the country's history and customs were remembered and honoured and that good generals and officials were rewarded, along with artists and scholars.

Nowadays rulers in democracies spend most of their time working as supporters of charities and good causes. They often set the style in **leisure** and fashion and get involved in the arts. In times of crisis a modern ruler sometimes has to get directly involved in politics to make sure the constitution is respected, as Juan Carlos of Spain (1975–) did in 1981, or to head off violence by getting groups in conflict to talk through their differences.

In democracies members of the royal families have lost almost all their power, but can still have great influence. The late Diana, Princess of Wales (1961–97), had no political position but her ability to attract media coverage helped to change public attitudes to AIDs victims and alerted people to the problem of land-mines. This photograph shows Diana with land-mine victims in Angola.

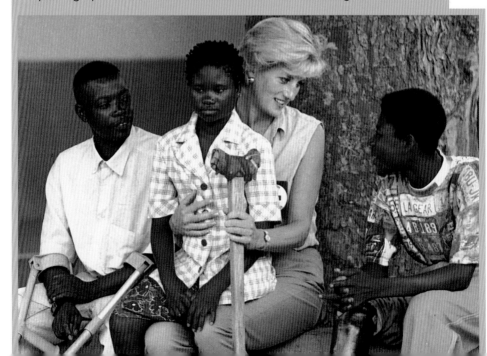

The way a monarch plays the part of ruler depends partly on what is expected of them, partly on their own personality, talents and tastes. Modern constitutional monarchies have strong institutions of government – parliaments to make the laws and officials, law courts and police to see that they are enforced and respected. This means that a ruler's personal qualities and abilities are much less important than when kings made all the key decisions. When kings made the laws or led armies in person their personality mattered very much. A healthy, energetic, clever monarch meant effective government. If they had many children the **succession** to the **throne** would be smooth and secure. If they failed to have an **heir** there might be **civil war**.

Sacred kingship – kings as gods, kings and God

Modern **republics** often treat government and religion as totally separate, but for most of history they have been mixed closely together. Rulers either claimed to be a god or to be acting for the gods on earth or at least to be able to deal with the gods. Egypt's **pharaohs** claimed to bring good harvests through religious ceremonies – but also stored up surplus grain in good years, to prevent starvation if harvests failed.

The gigantic statues of Egypt's pharaohs at Abu Simbel show their power. Ordinary people were not allowed inside temples. This separation marked the great distance between ruler and ruled.

God-kings existed in the ancient Near East 3,000 years ago. In America, the Aztecs of Mexico and Incas of the Andes had god-kings in the 16th century and in Africa they existed until the 19th century. Chinese emperors claimed to rule with the gods' favour, called 'the mandate of heaven'. Disasters in the form of invasions, floods, famine or epidemics, were interpreted as a withdrawal of that favour. **Rebellion** replaced the failed ruler with a new **dynasty**.

Kings as healers

Scrofula is an infection that creates ugly, painful swellings round the throat. It used to be known as the **King's Evil**. Sufferers believed the king could cure them by putting his hands around the swellings. This custom was brought to England by Edward the Confessor, who had seen it in France. In Britain, the last touching was for 200 victims in 1712, by Anne (1702–14). Touching for the King's Evil was last practised in France by Charles X (1824–30).

A 17th-century engraving showing King Charles II touching a man to cure him of the King's Evil.

King and church

Two thousand years ago, Rome's early emperors were worshipped as gods. Christians who refused to worship them were persecuted. Then in the 4th century AD the Emperor Constantine made Christianity the **empire's** official religion and emperors **persecuted** those who were not Christians.

This gold coin bears the head of the mad, murderous Emperor Caligula (AD 37–41) who demanded to be worshipped as a god – until he was **assassinated** by his own guards.

The Roman empire got so big that it was eventually divided into an eastern and a western half, ruled from Byzantium and Rome respectively. Byzantine emperors governed an area covering the modern states of Turkey, Greece and the Balkans. They battled for a thousand years to defend their Christian empire against **pagans** to the north and **Muslims** to the south. The last Byzantine emperor died fighting the Muslim conquerors of his capital in 1453. Russian rulers regarded Byzantium as a second Rome, the heart of Christianity after Rome itself fell to pagans.

After Byzantium fell, they proclaimed Moscow the third Rome and themselves as new guardians of the faith against pagans and Muslims. The Muslim rulers of the **Ottoman Empire** fought many wars against Russia, regarding themselves as defenders of the frontiers of their faith, **Islam**.

The western Roman empire broke up in the 5th century. Pagan and Christian kings fought for control of its lands. Christian rulers and the Church supported each other. The Church taught Christians to obey their kings and fight for them. The Church also supplied rulers with men who could read and write and serve as architects or doctors. In return, kings protected the Church, gave it land and fought against pagans and **heretics**. Kings who converted their people from paganism to Christianity, like Vladimir I of Russia (980–1015), were often made a saint by the church. So were kings killed in battle fighting pagans, such as Edward the Martyr of England (975–78) or Olaf of Norway (1015–30). Edward the Confessor of England was made a saint for being personally **devout** and very generous to the Church. St Louis IX of France (1226–70) was devout, generous to the Church, a persecutor of heretics and fought two **crusades** against the Muslims.

The monarch as moral crusader

Asoka (c. 265 – c. 238 BC) was an emperor of India. As a young man he loved war and conquest. Then he converted to Buddhism. Sickened by slaughter, he gave up making war entirely. He allowed other religions, founded hospitals and clinics, had wells dug and provided rest houses for travellers. Cruelty to animals was banned. He practised kindness to all and violence towards none. From India Buddhism spread throughout eastern Asia.

Defender of the Faith

Round the rim of every British coin is the name of the monarch, followed by the letters DG and FD. These stand for *Dei Gratia* (By the Grace of God) and *Fidei Defensor* (Defender of the Faith). British monarchs thus claim to rule with God's approval, a claim symbolized by the fact that at a coronation the ruler is given a crown, **orb** and **sceptre**, all topped by a Christian cross.

The title 'Defender of the Faith' was given to Henry VIII (1509–47) by the Pope for writing a *Defence of the Seven Sacraments*, which attacked the Protestant teachings of Martin Luther. When Henry VIII decided to make himself, instead of the Pope, head of the Church in England the king still kept the title.

This 16th-century portrait shows King Henry VIII, the monarch who was first given the title Defender of the Faith.

'Defender of the Faith' was later reinterpreted to mean defender of the English form of Protestantism – Anglicanism – which was therefore the opposite of its original meaning. At her **coronation** in 1953 Queen Elizabeth II (1952–) swore to defend the Protestant faith. Although the Queen is a regular churchgoer, in practice her position as 'Defender of the Faith' means little nowadays because no foreign power threatens to change Britain's faith by force, as Spain did in the 16th century. Some critics suggest dropping the oath, or changing it to 'Defender of Faiths' or ending the monarch's position as Supreme Governor of the Church of England.

A matter of conscience

In 1990 King Baudouin I (1951–93) of Belgium, a devout Catholic, gave up his throne for one day so that a law allowing abortion could be passed by the Belgian parliament without his having to approve it.

War and peace

Throughout history making war and peace has been one of a king's main tasks. Kings were defined by their personal bravery, strength and will to conquer.

Great warrior rulers inspired intense loyalty by their skill in arms and willingness to risk their own lives in battle. Military genius may create great **empires**, but is not in itself enough to maintain them. Alexander the Great (336–23 BC) conquered an empire stretching from Greece to India. The empire of Charlemagne (768–814) stretched to the borders of Spain and Denmark. The conquests of the Mongol Genghis Khan (1206–27) ran from Korea to Hungary. Each of these huge empires broke up after its creator's death because either no single **successor** was chosen or the heir did not have the political skills to hold it together.

Trying just to increase military power can strengthen or weaken a monarchy. The reigns of Peter the Great (1682–1725) in Russia and Frederick the Great (1740–86) in Prussia strengthened their countries. The dying words of Louis XIV (1643–1715) to Louis XV (1715–74), his successor as king of France, were, 'I have loved war too much; do not copy me in that'. But Louis XV was involved in several wars, each one producing ever-mounting debts. In the Seven Years' War (1756–63) France lost control of her lands in Canada to Britain. France's next king, Louis XVI (1774–92) supported American rebels against British rule out of revenge. French involvement in the American Revolutionary War (1775–83) broke the royal finances completely.

A military monarchy

The history of the English monarchy over a thousand years shows the varying importance of success in war and the changing part rulers play in it, from fighting in person to helping their people to keep up their spirits.

The execution of Louis XVI of France. The French political crisis created by royal bankruptcy led to revolution. A republic was established that aimed to spread revolution to its neighbours by force.

Richard I (1189–99) only ever spent five months of his reign in England, devoting his time to defending his lands in France and fighting in the Middle East. Fighting as a valiant **crusader** against **Islam** won him glory. He was called 'Richard the Lionheart'. Later, his unlucky brother John (1199–1216) lost his lands in France and was given the scornful nickname 'Softsword'.

Edward I (1272–1307) personally led the successful conquest of Wales, but his son Edward II (1307–27) was beaten by much smaller Scottish forces at Bannockburn in 1314.

In Robert the Bruce (1306–29) the Scots found a king strong enough to force England's rulers to accept the independence of Scotland in 1328. From 1603 onwards the two kingdoms had the same ruler. Scotland's parliament voted to merge with that of England in 1707.

The Hundred Years' War, which Edward III (1327–77) began when he claimed the throne of France, brought immense misery to both countries in the long run, but victories at Crécy (1346) and Poitiers (1356) made him hugely popular in England. Henry VIII inherited a mountain of money, but in trying to win glory like Edward III or Henry V (1413–22), wasted it all on pointless wars against France and Scotland.

As a woman, Elizabeth I (1558–1603) could not fight in person. But when England was threatened by Spanish invasion in 1588, she put on armour to rouse her troops with a speech of splendid defiance. This 17th-century painting shows Elizabeth among her troops at Tilbury.

James I lost popularity by ending expensive foreign wars, but by his political skills he kept England and Scotland united under his rule. Charles I (1625–49) lacked political skills so badly that he led the country into **civil war**. The prestige of the monarchy was still such that the leaders of the parliamentary army at first claimed to be fighting for the king – but against his bad advisers. The last British king to command personally in battle was George II (1727–60) in 1743 at Dettingen, now in Germany. Aged 60, he led a succesful infantry counter-attack against the French.

Leading by example

The idea that rulers should share common dangers with their people survived into the 20th century. King George VI (1936–52) toured bombed-out parts of London daily during the Blitz of 1940–41. The present Queen, then Princess Elizabeth, trained as a military driver in World War II. The Queen's second son, Prince Andrew, flew as a Royal Navy helicopter pilot during the fighting between the UK and Argentina over the Falkland Islands in 1982.

During World War II, when many European countries were overrun by Nazi troops, rulers kept up the morale of **occupied** peoples. King Haakon VII of Norway (1905–57) came to Britain, to head the Norwegian government in exile and broadcast to his people, encouraging them to believe in victory and to support **resistance**. Queen Wilhelmina of the Netherlands (1890–1948) personally congratulated every Dutchman who managed to join Dutch forces fighting from bases in Britain. King Christian X of Denmark (1912–47) stayed with his people, riding out of his palace daily on his horse to show that he was still there with them. When fighting began between the Danish resistance and the Nazis the king was imprisoned until the end of the war.

6 Ruling – right and wrong

What sort of ruler deserves, like Alfred, to be called 'The Great'? Great thinkers have been discussing how kings ought to rule for at least two and a half thousand years.

This 18th-century painting shows the Chinese thinker, Confucius (c. 551–479 BC). He argued that the ideal kingdom was like a pyramid of power in which everyone kept to his rightful place and the emperor set an example of correct behaviour by his hard work and wisdom. Government officials followed the emperor's example and the ordinary people under them followed their example.

In ancient Greece, the philosopher Plato (428–347 BC) believed the only people who ought to rule were the ones who did not want to, because they would not abuse their power. He also thought they should be trained in mathematics and other kinds of thinking so they could rule by reason rather than emotion.

Plato's pupil, Aristotle (384–322 BC), was less interested in what a government ought to be like in theory than in what actual governments were like in practice. He studied the constitutions of hundreds of Greek city-states and concluded that all systems of government fell into one of three categories – rule by the One, the Few, or the Many. In fact most systems combine all three.

Rule by	Good	Bad
One	Monarchy	Tyranny
Few	Aristocracy (the best qualified)	Oligarchy (a selfish few)
Many	Democracy (those chosen in elections)	Ochlocracy (mob rule)

The thousand-year history of ancient Rome illustrates a series of **transitions**. First the Romans had kings, then a republic, then emperors, who pretended that Rome was still a **republic**. These included emperors who were bloodthirsty **tyrants**, emperors who sincerely tried to rule for their subjects' happiness, and emperors who announced they were gods. Finally, Christian emperors proclaimed themselves the servants of the only true God.

The history of monarchies and republics in ancient Greece and Rome is important as the starting-point for the political theory and practice of all western civilization. It is doubly important because history is the storehouse of human experience. Succeeding generations turn to it for lessons and examples.

Modern-day senators

When the Founding Fathers of the USA were trying to devise a new form of government in the 1780s to replace the British monarchy they had rejected, they naturally turned to the ancient world for alternative examples. As educated 18th-century gentlemen, they knew Greek and Roman history well. It was quite natural that they should call their senior law-makers senators, like the senators of ancient Rome.

There are unavoidable weaknesses and dangers in any system of government which concentrates power in the hands of a single person. Serious physical or mental illness may make it impossible for a ruler to make sensible decisions.

Problems of power

'All power tends to corrupt, and absolute power corrupts absolutely.'

Lord Acton (1834–1902)

Assassination is a permanent danger, whether the assassin has political motives or purely personal ones. Rulers may simply abuse power to enrich themselves, to persecute critics or just because they enjoy the sense of power. When there is no person clearly chosen as a **successor**, **civil war** may break out between opponents who believe they have a right to take over. These problems can apply whenever power is concentrated in the hands of a single person, whether the system of government is a monarchy or a republic. Hitler and Stalin were both, in theory, elected heads of republics but in practice they ruled as dictators, abusing power on a far greater scale than almost any monarch has ever done.

Illness and madness

The recurrent madness of George III (1760–1820) was caused by a blood disease called **porphyria**. This may have been inherited from a distant ancestor, Charles VI of France (1368–1422), who also had it. George III's illness had only limited effects, because by his **reign** the king's personal power was limited. Politics carried on much as usual, with the king safely locked up and his son carrying out his ceremonial duties in his place.

Ludwig II of Bavaria (1864–86) virtually bankrupted his kingdom by building extravagant castles like this one at Neuschwanstein. Ludwig was finally declared unfit to rule.

It seems that drink and drugs inducing temporary madness, rather than madness in the clinical sense, accounted for the mass-murder of the royal family of Nepal in June 2001. After a quarrel caused by King Birendra's refusal to approve Crown Prince Dipendra's marriage to the girl he had chosen, Dipendra stormed out to return with a sub-machine gun. He murdered his father the king, and a dozen others, before shooting himself. He died shortly afterwards. King Birendra's younger brother, the killer's uncle, immediately succeeded to the throne.

Assassination

Assassination is murder that comes out of nowhere, rather than a deliberate execution like that of Charles I. An assassin may be inspired by political beliefs, like freeing his country from foreign rule, or may be driven by some personal grudge or thirst for fame.

There were six unsuccessful attempts on the life of Queen Victoria, all by lunatics. Presidents are even more at risk because they have real political power. Four US presidents have been assassinated – Abraham Lincoln (1865), James A. Garfield (1881), William McKinley (1901) and John F. Kennedy (1963).

This photograph shows Archduke Franz Ferdinand (rear right), **heir** to the throne of Austria-Hungary, on his fateful visit to Sarajevo in June 1914. His assassination led to an international crisis and the outbreak of World War I.

Abuse of power

The reign of Edward II of England is a case-study of how not to be a **medieval** king. Handsome and brave, but quite uninterested in soldiering, he preferred the company of actors and singers and liked to pass his time doing labourers' work like mending fences. Edward was bisexual and lavished lands, jewels and titles on his boyfriend, Piers Gaveston, who liked insulting Edward's officials and advisers. Gaveston was murdered by his enemies and so, eventually, was the king.

31

Machiavelli's methods

Many handbooks were written to tell kings how they should rule. Most told them to be generous, just and merciful. *The Prince* (1513), a famous book written by Niccolo Machiavelli (1469–1527), was brutally realistic. Machiavelli worked for the republican government of Florence until it was overthrown in 1512. He knew that real politics was full of blackmail, betrayal and murder. Machiavelli advised rulers to appear honourable, but act ruthlessly: 'The injury done to a man ought to be such that you do not need to fear his revenge.'

He warned rulers against being cruel for pleasure and advised them to make their subjects well off and contented. However, he also knew that rulers are faced with life-and-death decisions which ordinary citizens do not face. Therefore, to stay in power, they had to do things which would be quite wrong for a private individual because 'politics have no relation to morals'.

⑦ Kings under control

In very traditional monarchies kings actually rule – choosing chief advisers, leading armies and settling legal cases in person. The king is head of government, running the country, and head of state, representing its unity and dignity. The US president is both head of government and head of state. In modern **constitutional monarchies** and many **republics**, the two roles are separate. In Germany, for example, the president carries out ceremonial duties, such as presenting awards or meeting important foreign visitors, but the chancellor (the German prime minister) runs the government. In modern monarchies, like the UK or the Netherlands, the Queen reigns but no longer rules. She is head of state but no longer head of government.

This 19th-century painting shows a famous judgement made by the wise biblical king, Solomon, when two women both claimed the same baby.

Louis IX of France (1226–70) gave judgments in person, sitting in the open air under a tree, so anyone could approach him for justice. British judges still sit in court beneath a royal coat of arms, showing that, symbolically at least, the monarch is responsible for seeing that people get justice. European kings gave up being judges by the 1500s. But they were involved in law-making until the growth of **democracy** in the 18th and 19th centuries.

The British monarch's power to **veto** a law passed by parliament still exists in theory, but has not been used since 1707 because rulers have accepted that only an elected parliament has the rightful power to make laws. The Queen still retains the right, by custom rather than law, 'to advise, to encourage and to warn' the government about what it proposes to do and has a weekly private meeting with the prime minister for this.

Magna Carta

In England the idea that even the king must obey the law was confirmed when King John accepted an agreement known as Magna Carta (the Great Charter). John's reign was overshadowed by that of his brother Richard I, a brave and brilliant warrior. John's lands in Normandy were conquered by the king of France and he spent years trying to get them back. This meant raising money to pay for war and led John to abuse his rights to tax his subjects.

In 1214 John was defeated by France yet again, having set most of his own subjects against him. The leading barons rose in rebellion and forced him to agree, on 15 June 1215, to a written list of their demands. John had no intention of keeping his word, but pretended to, to buy time. He then renewed his war against the rebel barons, but died shortly afterwards. His son, a nine-year-old boy, became king as Henry III. Henry's advisers wanted to make a new beginning and thought it wise to reissue Magna Carta, to show that the new king would not abuse his powers.

From then on Magna Carta, at first an agreement to end civil war, became part of the law of the land. It was a safeguard for the rights of individuals and stood against **arbitrary** royal power. In the **constitution** of the USA and in the constitutions of many of its individual states can be found ideas and even whole phrases which can be traced straight back to Magna Carta. The most important passage promises, 'No free man shall be arrested or imprisoned or dispossessed of his property or outlawed or exiled or in any way damaged ... except by the lawful judgment of his equals or by the law of the land. To no one will we sell, to no one will we refuse, or delay, right or justice'.

England – Parliament gains control

Even strong kings like Edward I and Henry VIII realized that laws were easier to enforce if they were made with the co-operation of parliament. James I told parliament in 1609 that:

'The state of Monarchy is the supremest thing upon earth; for Kings are ... God's lieutenants ...' But, whatever he said, James I realized that he had to work with parliament. After Charles I had plunged the country into **civil war**, Charles II (1660–85) learned the awful lesson of his father's **reign** and aimed to get along with parliament rather than rule without it. Over the next century there were several further crises and conflicts between monarchs and parliament. They ensured that British rulers worked with parliament and in the last resort, parliament decided who was king. Britain developed into a **constitutional monarchy**, in which real power was increasingly held by ministers chosen from parliament. The French thinker Voltaire wrote admiringly, 'The English nation is the only one on earth which ... after repeated efforts, has established that beneficial government under which the Prince, all powerful for good, is restrained from doing ill'. Another Frenchman, Charles de Montesquieu, believed that the British had found the secret of good government by mixing rule by one, monarchy, with rule by few, the House of Lords, and rule by the many, the House of Commons, each balancing the power of the other two.

Absolute power

'... my orders would not be carried out unless they were the kind of orders which could be carried out ... I examine the situation, I take advice, I listen to educated people and so find out what effect my law will have ... when I am sure in advance of general approval, then I give my orders, and have the pleasure of watching what you call blind obedience.'

Catherine the Great of Russia (1762–96) explains to a government official that **absolute** power is not what it seems.

Absolutism in Europe

After France had been torn apart in the 16th century by religious wars in which Catholic fought Protestant, there was general support for a strong monarchy to restore unity and prosperity. The French parliament, the States-General, met for the last time in 1614. Under Louis XIV (1643–1715) France became an absolute monarchy, with few limits on the ruler's power.

This contemporary statue shows Louis XIV as a huge, muscular Roman hero. In fact he was rather small – but he had a big opinion of himself. He declared 'L'état, c'est moi (I am the state) and 'It is legal because I wish it'.

LOUIS XIV TERRASSANT LA FRONDE

The brilliant French court at Versailles, near Paris, dazzled Europe, inspiring rulers like the Russian Romanovs and the Habsburgs in Austria to become absolute rulers. In the end absolute rulers were unwilling to work with parliaments. This led to their violent overthrow by **revolution** in France (1789) and Russia (1917).

Revolution in Hawaii

King Kamehameha I (1782–1819) united the Hawaiian Islands into one kingdom. His successors tried to keep it independent as US missionaries brought in Christianity and the introduction of sugar-cane as a crop brought in Asian labourers and US businessmen. As native Hawaiians began to lose control of their own country, Queen Liliuokalani (1891–93) tried to use her position as monarch to limit political rights to her subjects. US residents formed an armed force to overthrow the monarchy and declared a republic. In 1895, Hawaiians loyal to the Queen rebelled to put her back in power, but the rising was crushed and the Queen was imprisoned. In 1898 the USA took over Hawaii as US territory.

Victorian Britain – monarchy in danger?

When Queen Victoria (1837–1901) came to the **throne**, the UK's monarchy was at a low point. George IV (1820–30) had been very extravagant when his subjects were suffering badly from poverty and unemployment. William IV (1830–37) was known as 'Silly Billy'. Victoria was just eighteen and people hoped for a new beginning. They were not disappointed. Victoria married her German cousin, Albert, had nine children and set a good example of happy family life. When Albert suddenly died of fever aged just 42, Victoria grieved deeply. For seven years she refused to go out. Critics said a queen who did nothing was pointless, and called for a republic.

In 1867 Walter Bagehot wrote a defence of monarchy, *The English Constitution*, arguing that Britain already was a republic – but it was still dressed up as a monarchy. Educated people knew that the Prime Minister and cabinet, chosen from the elected House of Commons, took the important decisions. The monarchy was still useful, though, because uneducated people did not understand how politics really worked. They could understand, though, the idea of a single person, sitting on a throne and wearing a crown, giving the orders. Bagehot believed that in a world of rapid change, monarchy created loyalty and pride among all British people.

Far more people, he said, were interested in a royal family than in politicians arguing with each other: '... royalty is a government in which the attention of the nation is concentrated on one person doing interesting actions'. Bagehot privately thought it unlikely the British monarchy would outlast the 20th century. Like many people, he expected republics would become the usual form of government everywhere. However, Bagehot's book became a textbook for future British monarchs.

A family crisis

When Victoria's popularity revived, it had nothing to do with books or politics but proved Bagehot's point about public interest in a royal family. In 1871 Victoria's eldest son, the Prince of Wales, fell ill with typhoid, the same sort of fever which had killed his father in 1861. For days he was on the edge of death. Ordinary people waited anxiously for news. His death would surely drive the Queen back into mourning and leave his little children fatherless. As Bagehot had said, this sort of family crisis interested most people much more than regular politics. When the Prince's fever broke the nation rejoiced. People and monarch had passed through a great emotional experience together and it had strengthened the ties between them.

As Victoria's children and grandchildren married into the royal families of Russia, Spain, Greece, Italy, Denmark, Romania, Portugal and Germany, she became the Grandmother of Europe.

The older she got, the more popular Victoria became. People liked the idea of a tiny old lady as the head of the world's most powerful **empire**. Victoria did little to make herself popular, but the strength of the monarchy rested on deeper historical forces. Giving the vote to ordinary working men led the UK towards democracy, but the continued existence of the monarchy made a link between the new style of politics and Britain's long history of rule under the law. Rather than being a break with the past, democracy could be seen as growing out of it. Victoria's long reign changed a traditional style of monarchy, interfering in politics, to a modern style in which the monarch is above politics, a symbol and focus of the nation.

Figurehead functions

Supporters of constitutional monarchy argue that it has definite advantages.

Efficiency

Being head of state and head of government is a double burden. Ceremonial duties like hosting banquets, reviewing troops, visiting colleges, giving out awards and opening bridges take up time that a head of government should be using to run the country.

Impartiality

Because an elected president is a politician, people who voted against him or her may not feel as loyal as they would if, like a monarch, he or she had no part in party politics. Many people honoured by an award say they would far rather receive it from the Queen, representing the whole nation, than the Prime Minister, who is elected by part of the nation.

Training

Monarchs spend a lifetime on ceremonial duties and can be trained from youth to practise the skills and self-discipline they will need. Albert Einstein refused to be President of Israel because he said he was no good at meeting people or making speeches.

Cost

A president who is a head of government as well as a head of state has real power and has to be surrounded with expensive top-level security. The cost of the British monarchy for the year 2000 was £35,000,000 – a little more than the £26,700,000 (not including secret service costs) it cost for US President Clinton to tour Africa for just six days in 1998.

The monarch as democrat

Modern constitutional monarchs normally stay out of politics, but in times of crisis they may have to intervene – even at the risk of their own position.

In 1967 army officers seized power in Greece. King Constantine (1964–73) went into **exile**. The officers abolished the monarchy but were themselves overthrown in 1974. One cause of this was that other countries did not want to deal with a government which ignored its democratic constitution – as the king had made clear by refusing to accept the military seizing power.

After a terrible civil war (1936–39) Spain was governed by the leader of the winning side, General Franco, as a **dictatorship** (1939–75). Franco arranged that Spain would go back to a monarchy. The grandson of the last king, Juan Carlos, became king in 1975 and immediately brought back democracy. When military rebels took the Cortes (Parliament) hostage at gun-point in 1981 the king personally ordered the armed forces to crush the revolt. He went on television to say he was defending the constitution and expected the armed forces to do the same. The example of Greece showed what the king was risking. The rebels backed down and the king's strong action confirmed his popularity with Spaniards of all political opinions.

In 1991 the military seized power in Thailand and altered the constitution so that the army, rather than the king, would choose the 270 members of the Senate. Encouraged by the king, mass demonstrations forced the military from power in 1992.

8 Kings in control

Monarchy normally links past and present, standing for the continuity of a society and its values and customs. As a source of their **authority**, kings often stressed how far back in history they could trace their family. This does not mean, though, that monarchy is always threatened by change. There are many examples of monarchs forcing change on reluctant subjects and leading change by personal example.

When European countries like Britain and the Netherlands first began to trade with Asia in the 16th century they had similar weapons and ships. However, from the 18th century the development of new technology in Britain made its ships and firepower far more effective. Britain became powerful and prosperous out of all proportion to its size, largely from the profits of global trade. Other monarchs tried to import changes to help their countries catch up. Their reforms often look as though they wanted to benefit their subjects and share power with them – encouraging trade, abolishing unjust taxes and promoting education – but their aim was national strength and efficiency, not **democracy**.

Peter the Great's greatest achievement was his new capital, St Petersburg, a port to serve as 'a window on the west' by bringing in foreign experts and technology and showcasing western lifestyles. This new focus for a new Russia was built by thousands of serfs, unfree labourers, who were literally worked to death.

Europe

Peter the Great of Russia (1682–1725) really was great – nearly seven feet tall and a human dynamo, eager to drag Russia out of the past. He learned modern shipbuilding in England and the Netherlands. Returning home, he brought in foreign experts to modernize his army, founded a navy and used both to conquer new lands in the south and west, in the Crimea and the Baltic.

Prussia, originally a cluster of poor lands scattered over what is now northern Germany, was transformed by the kings of the Hohenzollern **dynasty** into a great military power. The entire country was organized to support the army. Frederick the Great conquered the rich province of Silesia, encouraged industry and made Prussia strong enough to become the core of a future united Germany.

Vienna's huge Schonbrunn Palace symbolizes the grandeur of the rule of Maria Theresa (1740–86) and her son Joseph II (1780–90) who transformed their huge but disjointed central European territories into a strong, efficiently organized **state**.

Revolution delays reform

The French Revolution of 1789 led the armies of the revolutionary French republic to conquer most of Europe, destroying a number of monarchies and driving others into **exile**. As a result, most European monarchies were frightened of reform and opposed change for the next half century.

Asia

As Europeans used their technology and firepower to conquer colonies in Africa and Asia the traditional monarchies there had to choose resistance or reform. Eighteenth-century China was arguably the mightiest power on earth, with a population of 300,000,000 – 30 times greater than Britain's. China's rulers were so sure their civilization was superior that they ignored the advanced military technology of the west. China paid a terrible price in a series of wars which led to defeat and occupation at different times by British, French, German, American and Japanese forces. In 1911–12 a revolution overthrew China's last **emperor**.

Japan, which had traditionally admired China, learned from its failure and determined not to make the same mistake. The heads of the Tokugawa family had ruled since 1604 as shoguns (**military dictators**) in the name of the sacred emperor. In 1868 a group of young warriors overthrew the shogun. The **rebels** claimed they were restoring power to its rightful possessor – the fifteen-year-old emperor, who took the name Meiji (meaning 'enlightened rule'). The revolution became known as the Meiji Restoration. The new government rapidly modernized Japan under the slogan 'enrich the country, strengthen the army'. The modernizers brought in western experts and technology. However, the real drive for change came from the ruler's ministers, rather than from the ruler himself. By the time Meiji died in 1912, Japan had built up modern education and industry, defeated China and Russia in war and gained Taiwan and Korea as colonies.

The Middle East

Kingship, based on **tribal**, dynastic and religious loyalties, was the usual form of government in the Middle East until the 20th century. It has survived where monarchs have balanced tradition and change. The **Ottoman empire**, ruled from Istanbul, protected most of the Arab heartland from European colonization – and it did not seem much worth having, until the discovery of oil.

The Ottoman empire collapsed, following defeat in World War I, after six centuries of rule. Parts of its former territories came under British and French control. France, a **republic**, created new republics in Syria and Lebanon. Britain supported two new monarchies in Jordan and Iraq. Both ruling families claimed descent from **Muhammad**, the **prophet** of **Islam**. Their modernization was cautious, concentrating on building up modern armed forces rather

43

than improving conditions for their people. In Iraq this backfired and in 1958 the royal family was murdered and a republic founded. Since 1979 Iraq has been ruled by the military **dictator** Saddam Hussein. In Jordan the support of the well-disciplined army, recruited from tribesmen fiercely loyal to the throne, enabled the monarchy to survive the **assassination** of the first king, Abdullah, in 1951. King Hussein (1953–99) survived defeat in war and many assassination attempts, and passed on a stable country to his son and heir Abdullah.

Britain also had much power behind the scenes in Egypt, which was in theory an independent country. Its playboy king Farouk (1936–52) lived mostly abroad and took no interest in the welfare of his people. This led the army to overthrow the monarchy. In Egypt, as in Iraq, monarchy failed because it was seen as a tool of foreign interests, rather than as a defender of its own people.

Change came to the small tribal states of the Gulf region with the discovery of oil. This brought huge riches and an inflow of foreigners as experts, labourers and servants. Oman, the least oil-rich, has made the most progress towards democracy. Sultan Said bin Taimur (1932–70) opposed all change, even the abolition of slavery. He was finally overthrown by his British-educated son, Qabus bin Said Al Said (1970–), who realized the only way to keep power was to use it for modernization. Oman's limited oil wealth has educated its people and created modern jobs. In 1991 Quabus established a *Majlis al-Shoura* (National Assembly) which does influence political decisions. Other states ruled by sheikhs, such as Bahrain, Qatar and Kuwait, have used much greater wealth to provide welfare for their subjects (free housing, hospitals and schools) but have been nervous of creating assemblies with real power.

Kingship in Morocco has rested on the traditional religious **authority** of its monarchs, who still bear the ancient Islamic title 'Commander of the Faithful' and, like the rulers of Iraq and Jordan, claim descent from Islam's prophet, Muhammad. Morocco was divided and controlled by France and Spain from 1912 until 1956 and its rulers sidelined from power. Since then they have presented themselves as reuniters of the nation. King Hassan II (1961–99) established a constitution limiting his powers, but this was more in theory than in practice. Attempted uprisings in 1971, 1972 and 1985 were suppressed by force, but his **heir** has succeeded him peacefully as Muhammad VI.

Ibn Saud of Saudi Arabia and his followers were fierce followers of a particularly strict form of Islam, but he allowed the gradual and limited introduction of western technology, such as cars and telephones. His successors, enriched by massive oil incomes, have followed him in upholding Islam but limiting change. There are masses of cars – but women are still not allowed to drive them. Oil wealth gives Saudi rulers huge influence through generous development aid to poor Arab and Islamic nations. The country is run like a family business. Political power is shared out among the four thousand princes of the Saudi royal house. Saudi subjects receive many free benefits, but have no vote.

This picture shows four of the sons of King Ibn Saud of Saudi Arabia. Prince Feisal (centre) ruled as king from 1964 to 1975.

9 Monarchies today and tomorrow

In many parts of their **empire** in Asia and Africa the British found it cheaper and easier to govern indirectly through existing local rulers. As far as most Asians or Africans were concerned, the ruler they were used to obeying was still in charge. The British kept in the background unless the ruler abused his power. They rewarded good government with gifts and titles. Some rulers who had been only the **chief** of a small **tribe** took advantage of this system to become kings, ruling over much larger populations with British approval. This British system, called indirect rule, supported the survival of government by kings or tribal chiefs in areas as far apart and different as the Gulf, Jordan, Malaysia, Brunei, Bhutan, Nepal, Ghana, Uganda, Nigeria, Swaziland and Botswana. The French, by contrast, after giving up monarchy in favour of a **republic** in 1871, left republics behind them as the legacy of their colonial rule, from Mali in West Africa to Syria in the Middle East and Vietnam in South East Asia.

Taking turns

Modern Malaysia was created by the UK out of a dozen separate kingdoms. Since independence, the rulers have taken five-year turns to serve as *Yang Dipertuan Agong* (Supreme Head of the Federation).

The seven rulers of the United Arab Emirates elect a President and Vice-President from among themselves to head their federation.

Good works and good causes

Kings traditionally performed acts of charity as a matter of religious duty and example, whatever their faith. Typically this involved gifts of cash, food or clothes to the poor and setting aside lands to found places of worship or schools. Queens, where they were without political duties, were even more likely to devote time and treasure to good works. The charity tradition has continued into modern times and become much broader and less closely tied to religious causes, extending into the arts, business and the environment. Charity duties involve long days of travel, hand-shaking, speech-making and keeping up good humour.

As Princess Alice, Countess of Athlone (1883–1981) said, '... daily tasks, for months ahead, are ... set out in a diary of engagements from which only illness can excuse them. None but those trained from youth to such an ordeal can sustain it ... The royal motto *Ich Dien* is no empty phrase. It means what it says – I serve'. In terms of time, charity work is the main occupation of the UK's royal family today, involving over 3,000 visits a year to hospitals, schools, community centres, companies, art galleries and retirement homes.

The involvement of British monarchs in regular, non-religious charity work goes back at least to Charles II, who founded the Royal Hospital, Chelsea, for army veterans and the Royal Society to encourage science. Queen Victoria was patron of 150 charitable institutions and gave money to over 200 more.

This picture shows Queen Victoria presiding over the opening of the Great Exhibition in 1851. This was the first world fair. It was organized by Victoria's husband, Albert, to celebrate and promote peace, progress and prosperity.

Queen Elizabeth II has become involved in international projects, such as Voluntary Service Overseas; of the 3,200 organizations of which she is patron, some 500 are based or operate overseas.

In Spain today Queen Sofia heads a charitable foundation which helps drug addicts. Belgium's King Albert is especially interested in environmental problems and promoting trade. Denmark's exceptionally well-educated Queen Margrethe is very active in the arts. She has translated books from French and Swedish and as a practising artist has illustrated books, and designed postage stamps and scenery for the Royal Danish Ballet. Queen Beatrix of the Netherlands has a lifelong interest in the problems of the disabled.

Monarchy and identity

Queen Elizabeth II is head of state of over a dozen countries as well as the UK, including Canada, Australia, New Zealand and Jamaica. The Monarchist League of Canada defends monarchy on the grounds that its existence guarantees Canada an identity distinctive from its neighbour, the USA. 'We are already bombarded by American culture and the monarchy ... makes Canada unique.' Canadian monarchists also argue that a monarchy is actually more democratic and representative than an elected presidency because 'an elected president would owe his selection to a political faction and this would publicly divide him from many of his countrymen and would make his claim to represent the people less convincing'. French-speaking Quebec favours the monarchy because if it were removed it fears that the federal government might try to increase its powers over the provincial governments.

The accident of birth

'A king is a king, not because he is rich and powerful ... He is King because he is born. And in choosing to leave the selection of their head of state to ... the accident of birth ... Canadians ... proclaim their faith in human equality: their hope for the triumph of nature over political manoeuvre'.

Jacques Monet, Canadian historian

Queen Elizabeth II reviewing Guards in Ottawa, Canada in 1984.

Other arguments put forward by Canadian monarchists are:
1 The monarchy is largely paid for by the British taxpayer. Canadians only pay for the costs of the Queen's homecomings – less than a dollar per person a year. An elected head of state in Canada would cost much more than the resident Governor-General does.
2 Queen Elizabeth II's multi-national ancestry (34 identified nationalities, ranging from Albanian to Welsh) makes her particularly appropriate to represent a nation based on immigration.
3 By sharing its head of state with other countries, Canada promotes an outward-looking and global sense of identity appropriate for an interdependent world.

49

Republicanism in Australia

There have always been Australians, particularly of Irish Catholic descent, who disliked the monarchy. Large-scale post-war immigration from southern Europe and Asia has further weakened the traditionally British background of Australia's population to create a much more multi-cultural society.

In 1999 a **referendum** was held for Australians to decide whether to replace the monarchy with a **republic**, headed by a president. Anti-monarchists ignored the fact that for all practical purposes the head of state in Australia is the Governor-General, an Australian national who acts as the Queen's permanent representative in her absence. They argued that Australia had now grown up and should not have a foreign, non-resident head of state. A pro-royalist minority, mostly based in rural areas and consisting of older people, opposed the idea of a republic but the media, the young and the country's most influential writers were strongly in favour.

To the surprise of most political experts, the proposal was voted down. Some voters thought the monarchy simply was not a problem, persuaded by the 'if it ain't broke don't fix it' argument. According to the polls a dozen other issues, such as unemployment and health services, were ranked as more important. Most, however, rejected the particular arrangements on offer – an Australian head of state to be chosen by parliament. Instead they wanted a directly-elected People's President, rather than a Politicians' President. The politicians, however, objected to a directly-elected president on the grounds that this might make him a rival to the Prime Minister. For the present, therefore, monarchy remains.

An Australian alternative

In his book *Monarchists, Royalists and Republicans,* Geoffrey K. White proposes a way out of Australia's dilemma. He suggests Australia should give up British monarchy and establish its own system, but not become a republic.

White argues that an independent, resident Australian monarch is needed mainly as a guardian of the **constitution**, with reserve powers to act in a political crisis. The monarch might be called Head of State or Governor-General but would represent the Australian people, not the Queen. The Head of State would be chosen by an electoral college made up of holders of the Order of Australia, who have by definition been honoured for their contributions to national life. A small panel of twelve to twenty members of the college would be chosen at random to interview candidates and recommend one, who would then have to be approved by a two-thirds majority vote in parliament, or, more expensively, by a referendum. Politicians could reject an unsuitable candidate, but have no power to nominate one. The Head of State's reserve powers would not be defined but would include whatever was necessary to restore democractic government in a crisis. These powers would operate on the bee-sting principle – if the Head of State ever had to use them he would have to resign as soon as the crisis was over and make way for a successor.

Reforming the UK's monarchy ?

A 1996 pamphlet *Long to Reign Over Us?* written by the **Fabian Society** suggested the following reforms to the UK's monarchy:

- The Speaker of the House of Commons should approve Acts of Parliament instead of the Queen and read out the speech outlining proposed laws at the beginning of a new Parliament.
- The monarchy should be financed by a direct tax on each citizen (about £1.50 per year).
- A referendum should be held every ten years on whether the UK should keep the monarchy.
- New national **anthems** should be written for England and the UK.
- The rights and duties of the monarch and citizens should be defined by a written constitution.

51

- The monarch should cease to be supreme governor of the Church of England.
- Commonwealth Heads of State should take it in turns to act as Head of the Commonwealth and host the Commonwealth Heads of Government Meeting which takes place every other year.

The Fabian Society has often supplied policies for the Labour Party but the party has shown no interest in changing the monarchy. The only time the Labour Party discussed the future of the monarchy at its annual party conference was in 1923. The vote was ten to one in favour of keeping the monarchy, and the issue has never been raised since.

Comeback kings?

Simeon II of Bulgaria was just nine when a rigged poll ended the monarchy and forced him into **exile** in 1946. The king grew up to become a business expert, based in Spain. Bulgaria became a communist country and remained one of the poorest in Europe. In 2001, ten years after Bulgaria had finished with communism, it was still poor. Simeon returned from exile, ran for parliament and became prime minister with general support to crack down on crime and corruption and get the country going again. Simeon's appeal was that he was unstained by the past, owed no favours to anyone and was widely seen as an honest Bulgarian who wanted to do his best for the country. He denied intending to restore the monarchy: three-quarters of Bulgarians were opposed to this idea. If he does kick-start the country out of poverty, that proportion might well change.

Within weeks of Simeon's election victory, exiled ex-King Alexander of Yugoslavia was given permission to return from his adopted country, the UK, and live in a former royal palace in Serbia. Albania and Romania are other poor Balkan countries with exiles who claim their empty thrones. Could monarchy make a comeback in the Balkans?

10 So, what is monarchy?

Monarchy began as a form of government which almost always claimed to be divine in origin. For much of history, however, the power of monarchs depended on their success as warriors. Monarchs also drew on the personal loyalties of blood relatives or followers who they rewarded with powerful positions and land. Some monarchs have claimed **absolute** power, unchecked by any parliament or assembly, though even rulers who claimed to be absolute on earth usually accepted that religion set some limit to what they could do.

Beginning in Britain, monarchies have gradually become **constitutional**, ruling within a framework of laws established in co-operation with an elected parliament. The English revolutionary, Thomas Paine, once wrote that 'in America the law is king'. In practice this is also true in constitutional monarchies, so they are sometimes described as 'crowned republics', because real power rests with elected leaders.

Constitutional monarchs remain important as symbols of a nation's unity and self-respect. In times of political crisis they can safeguard the **constitution**. At times of national disaster they provide a focus for their people to rally around. Most of their normal working time is spent encouraging charity, education and other worthwhile causes.

A number of Asian, African and Middle Eastern monarchies are still unlimited by constitutions and parliaments. They may use their power wisely or badly but, without the link with their people that a constitution and effective parliament provides, they are less likely to be stable and successful in adjusting to change.

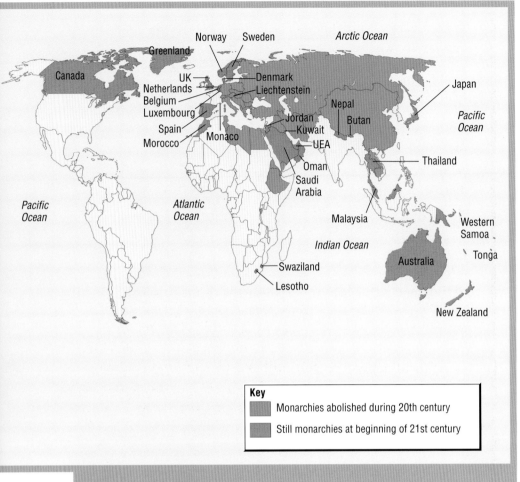

Key

■ Monarchies abolished during 20th century

■ Still monarchies at beginning of 21st century

World monarchies at the turn of 21st century.

The future of monarchy

Walter Bagehot thought that one day all modern countries would become **republics**. So far at least this has not happened. The monarchies of the Netherlands, Belgium, Norway, Denmark, Luxembourg and Japan survived defeat and foreign occupation in or after World War II. In Spain the monarchy was overthrown in 1931 and restored in 1975. Public support for the monarchy in the UK has fallen since the 1950s, but remains high. Polls conducted in April 2001 showed 70 per cent support for the monarchy and 19 per cent for a republic. Support for a republic is much higher among young adults than other generations.

A December 2000 poll showed 52 per cent thought the monarchy was important to Britain, but only 5 per cent thought the monarchy important to their own personal life. Asked to rank the monarchy's top priorities for the 21st century, 55 per cent said 'promoting British interests abroad', 43 per cent said 'working with charities', 34 per cent said 'attracting tourism' and 23 per cent said 'being head of the Commonwealth'. Another poll from the same month showed 63 per cent support for ending the ban on Roman Catholics succeeding to the throne. One in three people supported the idea of voting on who should succeed the Queen.

In Japan, Thailand and Malaysia there are no serious challenges to the position of the ruler. Other Commonwealth countries may follow Australia and consider replacing the monarchy with an elected head of state. The survival of monarchy in less stable parts of the Middle East, Asia and Africa will depend on the skill and luck of local rulers in adjusting to change. The long history of monarchy, the world's most common form of government for most of its existence, shows that monarchies which adapt survive.

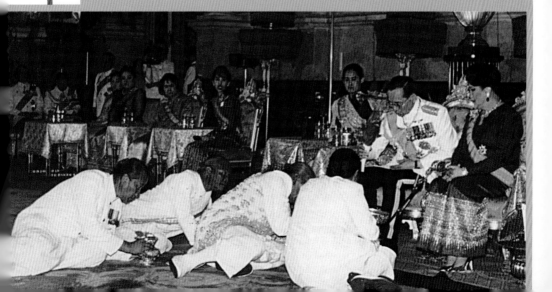

The royal court in Thailand, where the idea that the monarch is sacred in his person survives, and the king is still treated with immense respect.

Timeline

c. **3100 BC–AD 332**	Pharaohs rule Egypt
c. **1600 BC–AD 1912**	Chinese empire
c. **551 BC–479 BC**	Life of Confucius, Chinese teacher
428 BC–347 BC	Life of Plato, Greek teacher
336 BC–323 BC	Reign of Alexander the Great of Macedon, conqueror
27 BC–AD 476	Roman **empire**
AD 313	Roman emperor Constantine accepts Christianity
AD 768–814	Reign of Charlemagne
AD 871–99	Reign of Alfred the Great
1066	William of Normandy conquers England at the battle of Hastings
1206–27	Reign of Genghis Khan, founder of the Mongol empire
1215	King John accepts Magna Carta
1226–70	Reign of St Louis IX of France
1453	Byzantine empire ends with Ottoman conquest
1513	Publication of *The Prince* by Niccolo Machiavelli
1534	Henry VIII makes himself Supreme Governor of the Church in England
1643–1715	Reign of Louis XIV in France
1649	Execution of Charles I
1660	Restoration of Charles II
1682–1725	Reign of Peter the Great in Russia
1688	Britain's Glorious Revolution shows that parliament controls the monarchy
1743	George II becomes the last king of Britain to lead troops in battle in person
1775	British colonies in North America claim independence from the monarchy
1789	Revolution in France challenges the monarchy
1793	Execution of Louis XVI of France
1824–30	Reign of Charles X of France, the last king to touch for the **King's Evil**

1837–1901	Reign of Queen Victoria
1867	Publication of *The English Constitution* by Walter Bagehot
1868–1912	Reign of Japan's modernizing emperor Meiji
1897	Diamond Jubilee celebrations mark sixtieth year of Victoria's reign
1910	Monarchy overthrown in Portugal
1912	Overthrow of the last emperor of China
1914	**Assassination** of Archduke Franz-Ferdinand of Austria-Hungary starts World War I
1917	Revolution in Russia overthrows Tsar Nicholas II
1918	Collapse of monarchy in Germany and Austria-Hungary
1923	**Ottoman empire** abolished
1931	Collapse of monarchy in Spain
1932	Abdul Aziz Ibn Saud becomes king of a united Arabia George V becomes the first British ruler to speak to his people directly by radio
1946	Monarchy abolished in Italy Japan's emperor Hirohito declares that he is not a god
1947	Monarchy abolished in Romania
1953	**Coronation** of Queen Elizabeth II is the first to be televised
1975	Restoration of monarchy in Spain
1999	Australians vote to keep the monarchy
2001	Ex-king Simeon II is elected Prime Minister of Bulgaria Mass murder of royal family of Nepal Ex-king Zahir Shah of Afghanistan proposed to head new government

Further reading

C. S. Lewis, *The Horse and His Boy* (HarperCollins, 2001)

Fiona Macdonald, *Kings & Queens, Rulers & Despots* (Franklin Watts, 1995)

André Maurois, *Fattypuffs and Thinifers* (Jane Nissen Books, 2000)

J. R. R. Tolkien, *The Lord of the Rings* (HarperCollins, 1995)

David Williamson, *Brewer's British Royalty: A Phrase and Fable Dictionary* (Cassell, 1996)

Sources

Vernon Bogdanor, *The Monarchy and the Constitution* (Oxford University Press, 1995)

John Cannon and Ralph Griffiths, *The Oxford Illustrated History of the British Monarchy* (Oxford University Press, 1988)

Charles Douglas-Home, *Dignified and Efficient: The British Monarchy in the Twentieth Century* (Claridge Press, 2000)

Antonia Fraser, *The Lives of the Kings and Queens of England* (Weidenfeld & Nicolson, 1993)

Denis Kavanagh, *The Oxford Dictionary of Political Biography* (Oxford University Press, 1998)

Frank Prochaska, *Royal Bounty: The Making of a Welfare Monarchy* (Yale University Press, 1995)

Frank Prochaska, *The Republic of Britain 1760–2000* (Allen Lane, 2000)

Edgar Wilson, *The Myth of British Monarchy* (Journeyman Press, 1989)

Philip Ziegler, *Crown and People* (Collins, 1978)

Websites

abcnews.go.com/sections/world/DailyNews/monarchy020301.html

newssearch.bbc.co.uk

www.dailytelegraph.co.uk

www.guardian.co.uk/Archive/Article/0,4273,4394240,00.html

www.royal.gov.uk

Monarchies today

This is a list of existing monarchies, with the date of the monarch's accession in brackets.

Europe
Denmark: Queen Margrethe II (1972–)
Luxembourg: Grand Duke Henri (2000–)
Monaco: Prince Rainier III (1949–)
Netherlands: Queen Beatrix (1980–)
Norway: King Harald V (1991–)
Spain: King Juan Carlos I (1975–)
Sweden: King Carl XVI Gustaf (1973–)
United Kingdom of Great Britain and Northern Ireland:
   Queen Elizabeth II (1952–). As monarch of the United
   Kingdom the Queen is also Head of State of another dozen
   British Dependent Territories, including Bermuda,
   Gibraltar and the Falkland Islands. She is also Head of
   State of Canada, Australia, New Zealand, Antigua and
   Barbuda, Bahamas, Barbados, Belize, Grenada, Jamaica,
   Papua New Guinea, St. Christopher and Nevis, St. Vincent
   and the Grenadines, Solomon Islands and Tuvalu. The
   Queen is also symbolic Head of the Commonwealth with
   54 members, most of whom, like India or South Africa, are
   republics. Mozambique, a republic, asked to join the
   Commonwealth in 1995.

Asia
Bahrein: Amir Hamad bin Isa Al Khalifa (1999–)
Bhutan: King Jigme Singye Wangchuck (1972–)
Brunei: Sir Sultan Haji Hassanal Bolkiah Muizzaddin
   Waddaulah (1967–)
Cambodia: King Norodom Sihanouk (1993–)
Japan: Emperor Akihito (1989–)
Jordan: King Abdallah II (1999–)
Kuwait: Amir Jabir al-Ahmad al-Jabir al-Sabah (1977–)
Malaysia: Sultan Tunku Salahuddin Abdul Aziz Shah ibni Al-
   Marhum Sultan Hisammuddin Alam Shah (1999–2001)
Nepal: King Gyanendra (2001–)
Oman: Sultan Qabus bin Said Al Said (1970–)

Qatar: Amir Hamad bin Khalifa Al Thani (1995–)

Saudi Arabia: King Fahd ibn Abd al-Aziz Al Saud (1982–)

Thailand: King Bhumibol Adulyadej (1946–)

United Arab Emirates: President Zayid bin Sultan Al Nuhayyan (1971–)

Africa

Lesotho: King Letsie III (1996–)

Morocco: King Muhammad VI (1999–)

Swaziland: King Mswati III (1986–)

Pacific

Samoa: Chief Susuga Malietoa Tanumafili II (1963–)

Tonga: King Taufa'ahau Tupou IV (1965–)

Glossary

absolute without any limits

accession taking over as monarch

ancestor person from whom one claims descent

anthem a song of praise or gladness

arbitrary not controlled by law or reason

aristocracy rule by the best qualified

assassination planned murder of a person for political reasons

authority rightful power over people

chief leader of a tribe

civil war war between opposing groups within one country, rather than against foreigners

constitution set of rules for organizing a system of government

constitutional monarchy one in which the power of a monarch is limited by a constitution

coronation religious ceremony making a ruler the rightful monarch by giving him or her a crown

crusader person who goes on a crusade

crusades wars fought (1095–1272) by European armies to take back Christian holy places in the Middle East controlled by Muslim rulers

democracy government chosen by free and fair elections

descent having a person as a member of one's family in the past

devout sincerely religious

dictatorship system of government headed by a single person or small group, whose rule is based on force rather than free elections

dynasty family of rulers

empire large country or countries, including many different peoples

exile having to live outside your own country

Fabian Society a group of thinkers who put forward ideas for the British Labour Party

faction small group or party with strong beliefs

god-king king who claims he actually is a god

heir person given property or a position by someone who has died

hereditary passed on by birth

heredity order of birth

heretic person whose religious beliefs differ from those officially approved

illegitimate born to parents who are not married and therefore having no legal right to inherit their property or position

infantry soldiers who fight on foot

Islam religion followed by Muslims, based on the teachings of Muhammad

King's Evil a disease causing swelling of the lymph glands in the neck. It was believed that a monarch's touch could cure it.

legitimate born to legally married parents and therefore having the right to succeed to their property or position

leisure time off for recreation

literacy ability to read and write

medieval in the period of the Middle Ages, roughly AD 500–1500

military dictator dictator whose power depends on control of soldiers rather than a political party

multi-ethnic made up of different racial or cultural groups

Muhammad prophet who lived from about AD 570 to 632 and whose teachings became the religion of Islam

Muslim follower of Islam

occupied ruled by the army of a foreign country

ochlocracy rule by a mob

oligarchy rule by a selfish few

orb globe, usually made of precious metal and decorated with jewels, to symbolize the world

Ottoman empire Muslim empire which governed most of the Middle East and much of south-eastern Europe by 1530; it collapsed after defeat in World War I

pagan someone who believes in many gods, rather than one god as Christians, Muslims and Jews do

persecuted ill-treated or punished unjustly

pharaoh title of the ruler of ancient Egypt

porphyria hereditary blood disease which causes periods of mental illness

prophet person bringing a message from God

rebellion armed uprising against government

referendum vote for or against a single proposal

reign period of rule by a monarch

republic system of government headed by an elected president

resistance fighting back against an occupying army

Reims cathedral city in Normandy, north-west France

St Saint

scaffold platform for an execution

sceptre rod, usually of precious metal and decorated with jewels, which symbolizes a king's right to give laws and justice

Scone small town in Scotland where the coronations of Scottish kings were held

state an independent country

succession following on in a position of power

successor person who follows on to take up a position of power

traitor person who betrays his country

transition change from one situation to another

throne ceremonial chair sat on by a monarch, also a symbol of his authority

tribal based on a tribe, a group of people who believe they share common ancestors and do share a common language and customs making them different from other groups

tyrant absolute ruler with arbitrary power

verdict decision of a court

veto turn down

Westminster Abbey church in London where the coronations of English kings and queens have been held since 1066

Index

abdication 10
absolute monarchy 36, 53
Alfred the Great (King) 12–13, 28
assassination 29, 30–1
Australia 13, 48, 50–1

Bagehot, Walter 37–8, 54
Balkans 52
Belgium 20, 48, 54
Britain 4–6, 8–10, 12, 13, 17, 20, 22–6,
    29, 31, 34–5, 37–9, 40, 41, 43, 46,
    47, 51–2, 54–5
Bulgaria 52
Byzantium 7, 10, 18

Canada 13, 48–9, 59
Charles I (King) 4–5, 25, 35
Charles II (King) 6, 35, 47
China 16–17, 42–3
civil wars 7, 9, 29, 40
constitutional monarchies 11, 15, 33,
    35, 40, 53
co-rulership 10
colonialism 42, 46
coronations 6, 8, 20
Cromwell, Oliver 6

democracy 33, 39
democratic monarchies 11
Denmark 22, 26, 38, 48, 54
dictatorships 7, 11, 40, 43

Edward the Confessor (King) 8, 19
Egypt 7, 14, 16, 44
elected kings 8
Elizabeth I (Queen) 25
Elizabeth II (Queen) 8, 20, 26, 48,
    49, 59
Ethiopia 7
existing monarchies (21st century) 54,
    59–60

France 7, 8, 11, 17, 22, 23, 36, 42, 43,
    46

Germany 8, 25, 33, 38, 42
god-kings 16–17, 18
Greece 28, 38, 40

Hawaii 37
Henry VIII 21, 34
heredity, principle of 6, 8, 41

illness and madness 29–30
indirect rule 46
Iran 7, 11
Iraq 43, 44
Italy 38

James I (King) 4, 25, 34–5
Japan 7, 10, 13, 43, 54, 55
Jordan 43, 44

King's Evil 18

Magna Carta 34
Malaysia 46, 55
Middle East 43–4
modernizing 12, 13, 41, 42, 44, 45
Morocco 44–5

Nepal 30, 46
Netherlands 13, 26, 33, 48, 54
Norway 13, 26, 54

Oman 44
Ottoman Empire 10, 19, 43

parliament 6, 11, 34, 35, 53
Peter the Great 22, 41
pharaohs 7, 14, 16
political theory and practice 27–8, 32
Portugal 38
power
    absolute power 29, 35, 36, 53
    abuse of 29, 31

queens 7, 8, 10, 37, 38, 39, 46, 47–8

rebellions and revolutions 10, 17, 23,
    36, 37, 42, 43
reform 51–2
religion 16–18, 19–20
republics 6, 11, 13, 16, 23, 28, 33, 37,
    38, 46, 50, 54
Roman empire 8, 18–19, 28
Romania 38, 53
Russia 11, 18, 19, 22, 36, 41, 42

Saudi Arabia 45
Scotland 8, 24, 25
Spain 14, 40, 48, 54
succession 8, 9, 10, 11, 15, 29
Sweden 10, 13
symbols of power 8, 20

Thailand 40, 55
traditional and tribal monarchies 8,
    11, 42, 43, 46
tyrants 28

United Arab Emirates 46
United States 11, 31, 40

Victoria (Queen) 31, 37, 38, 39, 47

warfare 7, 21, 22–6, 29, 42–3
William the Conqueror 8–9